YOUR FAVORITE STARS

FEATURING

DUA LIPA

FACTS, QUIZZES, ACTIVITIES, AND MORE!

by Erin Falligant

CAPSTONE PRESS
a capstone imprint

This is an unauthorized biography.

Published by Capstone Press, an imprint of Capstone
1710 Roe Crest Drive, North Mankato, Minnesota 56003
capstonepub.com

Library of Congress Cataloging-in-Publication Data
Names: Falligant, Erin author
Title: Featuring Dua Lipa : facts, quizzes, activities, and more! / by Erin Falligant.
Description: North Mankato, Minnesota : Capstone Press, 2026. | Series: Your favorite stars | Audience: Ages 8-11 | Audience: Grades 4-6 | Summary: "What Guinness World Records does Dua Lipa hold? What was her first musical instrument? What are her hobbies? Dua Lipa's fans can learn the answers to these questions and others in this collection of fun facts, awesome photos, and more featuring the singing sensation!"—Provided by publisher.
Identifiers: LCCN 2025020371 (print) | LCCN 2025020372 (ebook) | ISBN 9798875255045 hardcover | ISBN 9798875254994 paperback | ISBN 9798875255007 pdf | ISBN 9798875255014 epub | ISBN 9798875255021 kindle edition
Subjects: LCSH: Lipa, Dua, 1995-—Miscellanea—Juvenile literature. | Lipa, Dua, 1995-—Juvenile literature.
Classification: LCC ML3930.L563 F35 2026 (print) | LCC ML3930.L563 (ebook) | DDC 782.42164092—dc23/eng/20250430
LC record available at https://lccn.loc.gov/2025020371
LC ebook record available at https://lccn.loc.gov/2025020372

Editorial Credits
Editor: Carrie Sheely; Designer: Elyse White; Media Researcher: Rebekah Hubstenberger; Production Specialist: Tori Abraham

Image Credits
Alamy: Barry King, 12, TCD/Prod.DB, 39; Getty Images: 45, Alberto E. Rodriguez, 6, Amy Sussman, 33, ARMEND NIMANI/AFP, 41, David M. Benett/Dave Benett, 22, Dia Dipasupil, 19, Dimitrios Kambouris, 14 (right), Emma McIntyre, cover, 16 (left), 32, Gareth Cattermole, 17 (background), 46 (middle), Jamie McCarthy, 30, Jason Koerner, 9, Joe Maher, 7 (bottom), John Shearer, 35, Kevin Winter, 5, 7 (top left), Matt Winkelmeyer, 31, Monica Schipper, 43, Naomi Rahim, 10, Rich Fury, 13, Rich Polk, 21, Vittorio Zunino Celotto, 36; Newscom: B4859/Avalon, 29, Collin Xavier/Image Press Agency ABACA, 37, Mairo Cinquetti/Pacific Press, 25, Pichichipixx/SplashNews, 27 (top right), SplashNews, 27 (left); Shutterstock: Anastasia Hum, 24 (middle left), ANNA ZASIMOVA (rainbow chrome star), back cover and throughout, BrightRainbow, 34, Chorna_black, 38-39 (stars background), Daddy_Kang, 27 (bottom right), David Ryo, 14 (bottom left), derter, back cover (chrome sparkle), lanastace, 42, Lightkite, 38 (film clapper), lilia_ahapova, 24 (middle right), M. Unal Ozmen, 28 (soda glass), Mashaart (silver star), back cover and throughout, Mintoboru, cover (planet), Nataly Studio, 28 (jalapeno), Pyty, 23, PxB, 11 (music notes), 16 (heart chat icon), SlipFloat, cover (shark fin), svekolka, 47 (bottom), Topuria Design, 47 (top), Tuba Reza, 18, v_kulieva (blurry heart background), cover and throughout, Valedi, cover (barbed wire heart), Visual3Dfocus, 17 (top right), vivat, 24 (top left), Yaran, 15, Yuliia Sobolieva, 21 (blue sparkle)

Printed and bound in China. 006461

TABLE OF CONTENTS

CHAPTER 1

A POP SENSATION

A one-of-a-kind name. A low, soulful voice. A dazzling stage presence. All of these have played a part in **DUA LIPA'S** success. She dreamed of being a pop star while posting covers of songs on YouTube at age 15. By age 29, she had released three albums and become one of the world's top female recording artists. Her songs have been streamed more than 45 billion times!

STAR SCOOP!

As a child, Dua tried out for the school choir—and didn't make it! A teacher told her she couldn't join because she couldn't hit the high notes. Now Dua appreciates her low voice because it sets her apart from other singers.

Dua performs at the Grammy Awards in 2024.

A RISING STAR

Follow Dua's path to success.

Future Nostalgia wins a Grammy for Best Pop Vocal Album

2021

2022

Kicks off *Future Nostalgia* tour

2023

Earns an acting role in the *Barbie* movie

2024

Releases her third album, *Radical Optimism*

Appears on the cover of *Time* magazine

Headlines at Glastonbury, Great Britain's biggest music festival

ABOUT THE ALBUMS

Dua recorded about 130 songs for her first album, ***Dua Lipa***. Only 12 made the cut! Her second album, ***Future Nostalgia***, was released during the COVID-19 pandemic. Dua hoped the songs would be played at clubs, but she had to livestream concerts from her apartment instead. The album had a retro disco sound. It inspired other artists to revisit disco too. Her third album, ***Radical Optimism***, was inspired by a breakup. Dua said, "It's about rolling with the uncertainties, being okay when things don't go your way."

STAR SCOOP!

Dua kept the name of her third album a secret before officially releasing it. While fans anxiously waited, they nicknamed the album "DL3."

Dua performing during the *Future Nostalgia* tour in 2022

NAME THAT SONG

How well do you know the lyrics of Dua's songs? Read these lyrics, and choose the song they are from.

1. "When the night's here, I don't do tears . . ."

A. "Dance the Night"
B. "Don't Start Now"
C. "One Kiss"

2. "I'm not here for long. Catch me or I go . . ."

A. "Cold Heart"
B. "Levitating"
C. "Houdini"

3. "Don't show up, don't come out . . ."

A. **"Break My Heart"**
B. **"Don't Start Now"**
C. **"Be the One"**

4. "I need someone to hold me close . . ."

A. **"Training Season"**
B. **"Break My Heart"**
C. **"Don't Start Now"**

5. "I've got you, moonlight, you're my starlight . . ."

A. **"Houdini"**
B. **"Levitating"**
C. **"Be the One"**

STAR SCOOP!

The song "Houdini" was inspired by magician Harry Houdini. After releasing the song, Dua Lipa held a dance party for fans at Houdini's Los Angeles estate!

Answers: 1. A, 2. C, 3. B, 4. A, 5. B

CHAPTER 2

FRIENDS AND FANS

Dua recorded a song with musical legend Elton John. She has performed with him onstage and even gets together with him for dinner parties. He said, "We're great friends, and I adore her."

Posters announcing the single Dua Lipa recorded with Elton John

Dua has also cowritten songs with superstars Chris Martin of Coldplay, Miley Cyrus, and Megan Thee Stallion. For her album **Radical Optimism**, Dua worked with a small team of cowriters. She called it one of the best experiences of her life. "We're all so proud of this project," she said. "It was like our baby."

STAR SCOOP!

Dua's cowriters say she's a perfectionist, and Dua admits it's true! She rewrites lines over and over again until they feel *just* right.

MAKE A "DUA DOODLES" NOTEBOOK

Dua writes her songs in a thick notebook she bought from a drugstore. The pages are covered in notes, lyrics, and doodles. You can create art with friends just like Dua does!

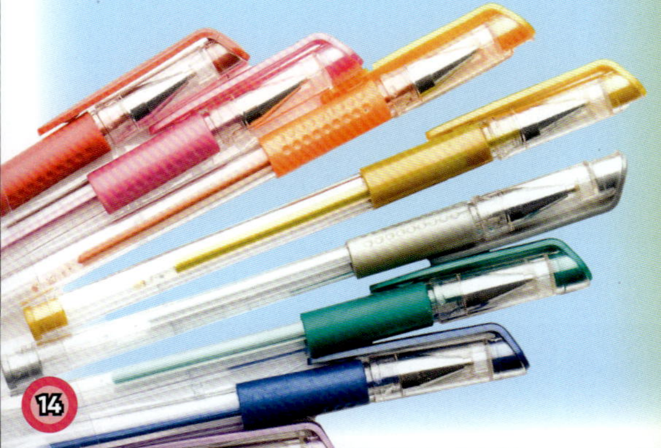

WHAT YOU DO:

1. Choose a notebook, and decorate the cover with your friend. Create a collage of stickers or cut-out images, and add gems or other accessories. Tie a ribbon to the wire binding.

2. Find a few sparkly gel pens, markers, or colored pencils.

3. Start your masterpiece. It could be a sketch, a doodle, or the first few lines of a song or poem.

4. Pass the notebook to your friend, and give them time to add to your creation.

5. Pass the notebook back and forth until one of you declares the masterpiece "done." Then turn the page, and start something new!

A SOCIAL MEDIA SUPERSTAR

Dua is incredibly popular on social media. By the end of 2024, she had more than 87 million followers on Instagram and more than 10 million on TikTok. She was the youngest female artist to reach 1 billion views for a video on YouTube. And in 2021, Dua set a Guinness World Record for the most monthly listeners for a female artist on Spotify. She had more than 65 million monthly listeners!

STAR SCOOP!

When Dua won a Grammy for Best New Artist, she thanked her fans. She said they "have allowed me to be the best version of myself."

CHAPTER 3

GROWING UP DUA

TRUE OR FALSE

Test your Dua Lipa IQ! Is each statement true or false?

1. Dua grew up speaking two different languages.
2. She was born in Albania.
3. She has a brother and a sister.
4. Dua's mom was in a rock band.
5. Dua's toughest subjects in school were science and math.

6. She worked as a teenager waiting tables.

7. She attended modeling school.

Answers
1. True. She speaks English and Albanian.
2. False. She was born in London.
3. True.
4. False. Her dad was, though!
5. True.
6. True.
7. False. She attended theater school.

HOW'D YOU DO?

6-7 correct: **TOP FAN**
4-5 correct: **TUNED IN**
1-3 correct: **MORE TO LEARN (READ ON!)**

WHAT'S IN A NAME?

Dua's first name means "love" in Albanian, but Dua didn't love her name as a child. She said in 2019, "I just wanted a normal name: Sarah, Hannah, Chloe, anything, I'll take it." Dua is proud of her name now, even though it's sometimes mispronounced. A talk show host accidentally called her "Dula Peep" during an interview, and the nickname stuck! Another nickname, which started on TikTok, is "Lipa Dupa." Whatever she's called, one thing is certain: Dua has made a true name for herself on the music scene.

STAR SCOOP!

Between 2017 and 2019, the number of babies in England named "Dua" doubled! That's when Dua's song "New Rules" hit number one on the charts there.

TWO HOMES

Dua's parents lived in **Kosovo** in southeastern Europe until 1992, when the Bosnian war broke out. They moved to **London, England**, where Dua and her siblings were born. After the war ended, the family moved back to Kosovo. But when Dua was 15, she persuaded her parents to let her return to London to finish school. She thought London was the best place to pursue a music career. This turned out to be a great idea. A few years later, she signed on with a record label. The rest is history!

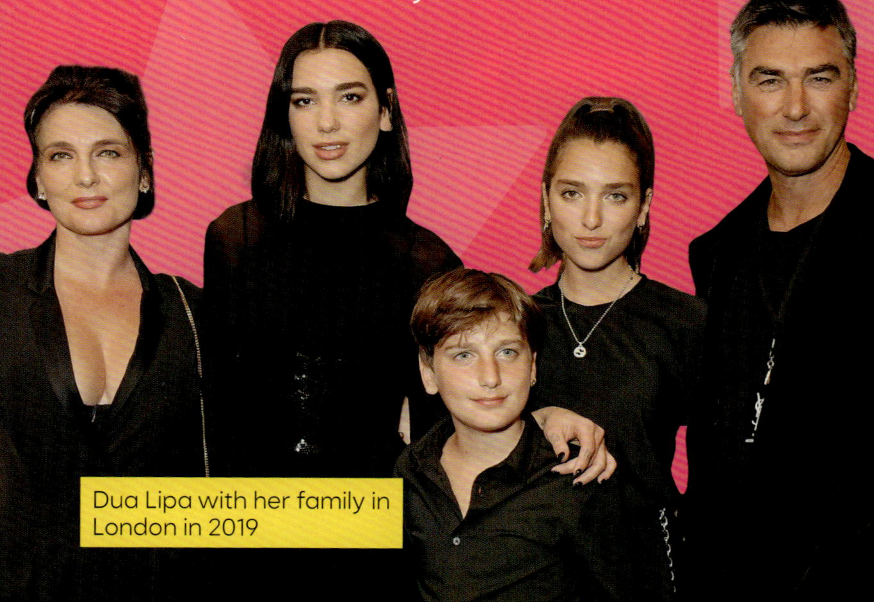

Dua Lipa with her family in London in 2019

STAR SCOOP!

Dua attended singing school in London with a teacher named Ray. "He heard my really deep voice. He was like, 'You've got something special. Use it,'" she later said. "He completely changed my life."

MUSICAL FIRSTS

There's a first time for everything, even for Dua!

FIRST ALBUM SHE OWNED AS A KID: NELLY FURTADO'S *WHOA, NELLY!*

FIRST SITE SHE POSTED ORIGINAL SONGS ON: SOUNDCLOUD

FIRST SINGLE: "NEW LOVE"

FIRST SITE SHE POSTED COVER SONGS ON: YOUTUBE

FIRST MUSICAL IDOLS: PINK, NELLY FURTADO, AND HER OWN DAD (A MUSICIAN!)

FIRST INSTRUMENT: THE CELLO

FIRST U.S. TOUR: HER SELF-TITLED TOUR 2017–2018

STAR SCOOP!

Fifteen-year-old Dua was nervous to post her first cover song online. But she posted it anyway. "You just have to do the thing that you love, and I'm so glad I did," she said later.

CHAPTER 4

FAVORITE THINGS

Dua has said, "I love my music career . . . but it's not the only thing I am." What else does she love to do? Stay on top of art, music, and movies. Catch up on reading. Eat out at restaurants, shop, and travel! Dua created a website called **Service95** with tips about the things she loves and advice for helping those in need. "Sometimes, you want to help but you don't really know how to help. I want to help give young people the tools to make a difference," said Dua.

STAR SCOOP!

Service95 wasn't Dua's first lifestyle website. She had her own blog as a teenager called "Dua Daily." She shared style tips and recipes.

Dua shopping in London

DUA THE FOODIE

"I'm obsessed with food," Dua says. "If I can just do little **food trips** and just go eat and try different things . . . that's the dream." Her mom is Albanian, and her recipes are some of Dua's favorite comfort foods. Dua loves pita bread, byrek (a flaky pastry with filling), spinach pie, and sujuk (a spicy sausage). She enjoys cooking for family and friends too. Her specialty is her "famous" roast chicken with beet roots and leeks.

STAR SCOOP!

Some of Dua's recipes have gone viral, but not all are hits. She got mixed reviews for her ice cream topped with olive oil and sea salt and for her diet cola mixed with olive juice and jalapeños.

TEN OF DUA'S FAMOUS FASHIONS

1. a bold dress with a giant waist bow (Met Gala 2019)

2. a black hooded jumpsuit (Paris Fashion Week 2023)

3. a classic white ball gown (Met Gala 2023)

4. a butterfly-print slip dress (*Barbie* premiere in London 2023)

5. a shimmery pink crop top and wrap skirt (Milan Fashion Week 2022)

6. a black gown with a strappy bodice (Grammy Awards 2022)

7. a white silky slip dress (Grammy Awards 2020)

8. a sparkly "disco ball" dress (Grammy Awards 2024)

9. a sparkly silver-sequined gown (Elton John AIDS Foundation party 2021)

10. an elegant long-sleeved crepe gown (Fashion Awards 2021)

STAR SCOOP!

Dua is a fashionista! She sometimes walks the runway in Versace fashions. She even helped friend Donatella Versace design a collection of clothing.

DECODE THE TATTOOS

Dua loves tiny tattoos. Here's what some of her tattoos mean:

PALM TREE: REPRESENTING LOS ANGELES

"R" AND "G": SIBLINGS RINA AND GJIN

"THIS MEANS NOTHING": DUA SAYS THIS ONE WAS JUST FOR FUN!

NUMBER 7: IN HONOR OF SOCCER STAR CRISTIANO RONALDO

"ANGEL": ON DUA'S SHOULDER TO WATCH OVER HER

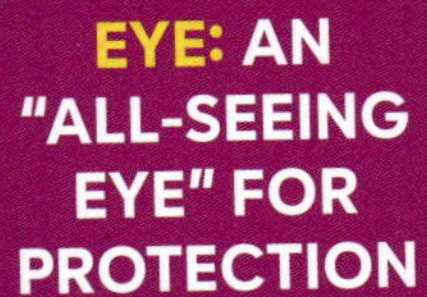

EYE: AN "ALL-SEEING EYE" FOR PROTECTION

"245": THE NUMBER OF SHOWS IN HER FIRST TOUR

"SUNNY HILL": WHERE HER PARENTS GREW UP IN KOSOVO

STEMMED ROSE: "95"—THE YEAR DUA WAS BORN—IS HIDDEN IN THE LEAF!

ARABIC WRITING: MEANS "LOVE" IN ENGLISH

BARBED-WIRE HEART: A REMINDER TO PROTECT HER HEART

CHAPTER **5**

SAVVY IN BUSINESS

Dua is a smart businesswoman. She started her own production and publishing company called **Radical22 Publishing**. Through it, she supports projects that matter to her. "Through my book club, I get sent lots of new books," she says, "and if I find a story that I love, then maybe I can help produce it or bring it into a different world." She produced a documentary about the music scene in Camden, her neighborhood in London. She also started a podcast so that she could interview people who inspire her.

STAR SCOOP!

Dua has interviewed more than 40 people for her podcast, ***Dua Lipa: At Your Service***. Famous guests included Apple CEO Tim Cook, musician Billie Eilish, and Greta Gerwig, director of the ***Barbie*** movie.

PARTNERING WITH BIG BRANDS

Part of Dua's business is being a **brand ambassador**, or a celebrity who backs products and helps them sell. She has represented more than 12 different brands! What kinds of brands? Everything from cars and athletic wear to fashion and fragrance.

FASHION
- PEPE JEANS
- VERSACE
- MUGLER
- CHANEL

BEAUTY AND FRAGRANCE
- MAC COSMETICS
- REVLON
- YVES SAINT LAURENT

JEWELRY
- TIFFANY & CO.

BEVERAGE
- EVIAN MINERAL WATER

LIGHTS . . . CAMERA . . . ACTION!

Dua is an actor as well as a musician. In 2023, she made her acting debut as **Mermaid Barbie** in the ***Barbie*** movie. Dua loved the colorful wigs she wore! She said, "It reminded me of how much I used to love playing dress-up as a kid." A year later, she played a spy named Lagrange in the comedy movie ***Argylle***. She had no acting lessons for either role. She just tried to be herself on camera. And for ***Argylle***, she did a lot of her own stunts!

STAR SCOOP!

Dua wrote and recorded a song for the ***Barbie*** soundtrack. "Dance the Night" was nominated for two Grammy Awards: Song of the Year and Best Song Written for Visual Media.

CHAPTER 6

GIVING BACK

Dua uses her fame and her Service95 website to raise money and awareness for many different causes. She supports **refugees** who had to leave their homes because of violence, war, or natural disasters. She fights for women's and children's rights all over the world. And with her father, she created the **Sunny Hill Festival** to raise money for charity in their home country. The money from the festival goes to the Sunny Hill Foundation to help young people in Kosovo who are in need.

STAR SCOOP!

Dua feels empathy for refugees because her own parents had to flee Kosovo due to war. She said, "From my experience of being in Kosovo and understanding what war does, no one really wants to leave their home."

Dua performing at the Sunny Hill Festival

SEVEN WAYS DUA HAS HELPED OTHERS

1. PERFORMED IN A FUNDRAISER FOR PEOPLE WHO ARE UNHOUSED IN LONDON

2. VISITED REFUGEE CHILDREN IN LEBANON WITH THE UNITED NATIONS CHILDREN'S FUND (UNICEF)

3. PERFORMED IN A FUNDRAISER FOR FEED THE CHILDREN

4. RAFFLED OFF THE MANUSCRIPT OF HER SONG "DON'T START NOW" TO FIGHT CHILDHOOD CANCER

5. PERFORMED IN A FUNDRAISER FOR THE ELTON JOHN AIDS FOUNDATION

6. PARTNERED WITH GLOBAL CITIZEN TO HELP END WORLDWIDE POVERTY

7. ASKED FANS ON INSTAGRAM TO SUPPORT VICTIMS OF FLOODS AND AN EARTHQUAKE

Dua performing at a UNICEF fundraiser

STAR SCOOP!

For UNICEF's "Go Blue" campaign, Dua starred in a YouTube video. She called herself "Bluea Lipa" and changed some lyrics of "Be the One" from "red" to "blue."

PROVIDING DURING THE PANDEMIC

During the COVID-19 pandemic, Dua asked fans to donate money to help refugees living in crowded places. She performed "**Don't Start Now**" from her apartment on a TV special called "**Homefest**." It raised money for the Centers for Disease Control. She performed "Break My Heart" on another TV special. It supported high school students who couldn't attend prom or graduation ceremonies because of COVID-19. She was also a part of "Live Lounge Allstars," musicians who recorded songs from home to encourage social distancing.

STAR SCOOP!

Dua was nicknamed the "Quarantine Queen" after releasing her third album at the start of the pandemic. She hoped her music helped people by providing a soundtrack for their workouts and kitchen dance parties.

Dua Lipa performs on TV in 2020 to support high school students.

STAR SCOOP!

After an earthquake in Albania in 2019, Dua worked with fashion designers to create "Pray for Albania" T-shirts. They were sold to raise money for survivors.

DESIGN A TEE

Be like Dua! Design a shirt to support a cause you care about. Here's how:

- Get a white T-shirt and fabric markers.
- Think of a cause that matters to you, such as finding homes for pets or protecting the environment.
- Come up with a slogan to write on your T-shirt, such as"Protect the Planet" or "Find Your Fur-ever Friend."
- Add patterns or pictures. Can you add paw prints on the sleeves? Ocean waves along the hemline?
- Add color that matches your theme, such as green for the environment. Anything goes—you're the designer!

ABOUT THE AUTHOR

Erin Falligant has written more than 50 books for children. Her Joss series for American Girl, written about a young surfer with hearing loss, earned a 2020 Moonbeam Gold Medal Award. Erin draws from her master's degree in child clinical psychology to write advice books on changing bodies, standing up to bullies, making friends, and mastering mindfulness. To learn more about Erin and her books, visit www.erinfalligant.com

READ MORE ABOUT YOUR FAVORITE STARS!

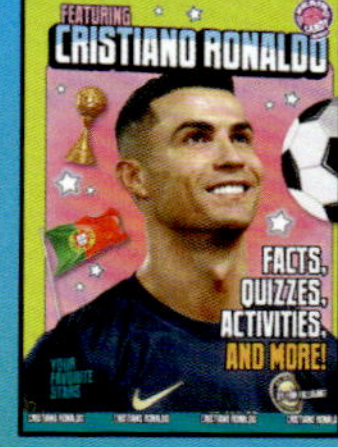

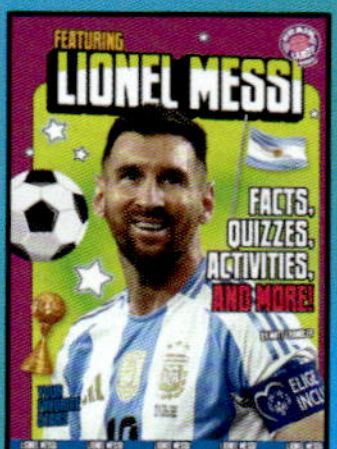